# 5 Minute Gratitude Journal

*This 5 Minute Gratitude Journal Belongs To*

_____

Day _____ Date _____

Today I am **Grateful** for:

_____

_____

_____

_____

_____

_____

*"Do not spoil what you have by desiring what you have not; remember that what you now have was once among the things you only hoped for."— Epicurus*

Day _____ Date _____

Today I am **Grateful** for:

_____

_____

_____

_____

_____

_____

_____

Day _____ Date _____

Today I am **Grateful** for:

_____

_____

_____

_____

_____

_____

*"Let gratitude be the pillow upon which you kneel to say
your nightly prayer. And let faith be the bridge you
build to overcome evil and welcome good."*
— Maya Angelou

Day _____ Date _____

Today I am **Grateful** for:

_____

_____

_____

_____

_____

_____

_____

Day _____  Date _____

Today I am **Grateful** for:

_____

_____

_____

_____

_____

_____

*"Acknowledging the good that you already have in your life is the foundation for all abundance."*
*— Eckhart Tolle*

Day _____  Date _____

Today I am **Grateful** for:

_____

_____

_____

_____

_____

_____

Day _____ Date _____

Today I am **Grateful** for:

_____

_____

_____

_____

_____

_____

"Forget yesterday - it has already forgotten you.
Don't sweat tomorrow - you haven't even met.
Instead, open your eyes and your heart to a truly
precious gift - today."
— Steve Maraboli

Day _____ Date _____

Today I am **Grateful** for:

_____

_____

_____

_____

_____

_____

Day _____ Date _____

Today I am **Grateful** for:

_____

_____

_____

_____

_____

_____

*"Some people grumble that roses have thorns; I am
grateful that thorns have roses."*
*— Alphonse Karr*

Day _____ Date _____

Today I am **Grateful** for:

_____

_____

_____

_____

_____

_____

Day _____ Date _____

Today I am **Grateful** for:

_____

_____

_____

_____

_____

_____

*"Gratitude is not only the greatest of virtues, but the parent of all others."*
— *Marcus Tullius Cicero*

Day _____ Date _____

Today I am **Grateful** for:

_____

_____

_____

_____

_____

_____

_____

Day _____ Date _____

Today I am **Grateful** for:

_____

_____

_____

_____

_____

_____

*"God gave you a gift of 86 400 seconds today. Have*
*you used one to say thank you "*
*— William Arthur Ward*

Day _____ Date _____

Today I am **Grateful** for:

_____

_____

_____

_____

_____

_____

_____

Day _____ Date _____

Today I am **Grateful** for:

_____

_____

_____

_____

_____

_____

*"Gratitude looks to the Past and love to the Present;*
*fear, avarice, lust, and ambition look ahead."*
*— C.S. Lewis*

Day _____ Date _____

Today I am **Grateful** for:

_____

_____

_____

_____

_____

_____

Day _____ Date _____

Today I am **Grateful** for:

_____

_____

_____

_____

_____

_____

"I would maintain that thanks are the highest form
of thought; and that gratitude is happiness doubled
by wonder". ~G.K. Chesterton

Day _____ Date _____

Today I am **Grateful** for:

_____

_____

_____

_____

_____

_____

_____

Day _____ Date _____

Today I am **Grateful** for:

-------------------------------------------------

-------------------------------------------------

-------------------------------------------------

-------------------------------------------------

-------------------------------------------------

-------------------------------------------------

*"When you are grateful, fear disappears and
abundance appears."*
*— Anthony Robbins*

Day _____ Date _____

Today I am **Grateful** for:

-------------------------------------------------

-------------------------------------------------

-------------------------------------------------

-------------------------------------------------

-------------------------------------------------

-------------------------------------------------

Day _____ Date _____

Today I am **Grateful** for:

_____

_____

_____

_____

_____

_____

*"Feeling gratitude and not expressing it is like
wrapping a present and not giving it."*
*— William Arthur Ward*

Day _____ Date _____

Today I am **Grateful** for:

_____

_____

_____

_____

_____

_____

_____

Day _____ Date _____

Today I am **Grateful** for:

_____

_____

_____

_____

_____

_____

"The world is 3 days: As for yesterday, it has vanished along with all that was in it. As for tomorrow, you may never see it. As for today, it is yours, so work on it." — al-Hasan al-Basri

Day _____ Date _____

Today I am **Grateful** for:

_____

_____

_____

_____

_____

_____

_____

Day _____ Date _____

Today I am **Grateful** for:

_____

_____

_____

_____

_____

_____

*"After every storm, there is a rainbow. If you have
eyes, you will find it. If you have wisdom, you will
create it. If you have love for yourself and others, you
won't need it." — Shannon L. Alder*

Day _____ Date _____

Today I am **Grateful** for:

_____

_____

_____

_____

_____

_____

Day _____ Date _____

Today I am **Grateful** for:

_____

_____

_____

_____

_____

_____

*"Regardless of Sunshine or Rain, Be Thankful for
another GREAT day…and treat Life as the
ULTIMATE Gift…. Because IT IS :)"*
— *Pablo*

Day _____ Date _____

Today I am **Grateful** for:

_____

_____

_____

_____

_____

_____

Day _____ Date _____

Today I am **Grateful** for:

_____

_____

_____

_____

_____

_____

*"The unthankful heart discovers no mercies; but the thankful heart will find, in every hour, some heavenly blessings." — Henry Ward Beecher*

Day _____ Date _____

Today I am **Grateful** for:

_____

_____

_____

_____

_____

_____

_____

Day _____ Date _____

Today I am **Grateful** for:

------------------------------------------------

------------------------------------------------

------------------------------------------------

------------------------------------------------

------------------------------------------------

------------------------------------------------

"For each new morning with its light,
For rest and shelter of the night,
For health and food, for love and friends,
For everything Thy goodness sends."
— Ralph Waldo Emerson

Day _____ Date _____

Today I am **Grateful** for:

------------------------------------------------

------------------------------------------------

------------------------------------------------

------------------------------------------------

------------------------------------------------

------------------------------------------------

Day _____ Date _____

Today I am **Grateful** for:

_____

_____

_____

_____

_____

_____

*"When it comes to life the critical thing is whether you take things for granted or take them with gratitude."*
— G.K. Chesterton

Day _____ Date _____

Today I am **Grateful** for:

_____

_____

_____

_____

_____

_____

Day _____ Date _____

Today I am **Grateful** for:

_____

_____

_____

_____

_____

_____

*"Take full account of what Excellences you possess,
and in gratitude remember how you would hanker
after them, if you had them not."*
— Marcus Aurelius

Day _____ Date _____

Today I am **Grateful** for:

_____

_____

_____

_____

_____

_____

Day _____ Date _____

Today I am **Grateful** for:

---------------------------------------------------------------

---------------------------------------------------------------

---------------------------------------------------------------

---------------------------------------------------------------

---------------------------------------------------------------

---------------------------------------------------------------

*"I may not be where I want to be but I'm thankful for not being where I used to be."*
*— Habeeb Akande*

Day _____ Date _____

Today I am **Grateful** for:

---------------------------------------------------------------

---------------------------------------------------------------

---------------------------------------------------------------

---------------------------------------------------------------

---------------------------------------------------------------

---------------------------------------------------------------

Day _____ Date _____

Today I am **Grateful** for:

_____

_____

_____

_____

_____

_____

*"The miracle is not to walk on water. The miracle is to walk on the green earth, dwelling deeply in the present moment and feeling truly alive."*
*— Thích Nhất Hạnh*

Day _____ Date _____

Today I am **Grateful** for:

_____

_____

_____

_____

_____

_____

Day _____ Date _____

Today I am **Grateful** for:

-------------------------------------------------------

-------------------------------------------------------

-------------------------------------------------------

-------------------------------------------------------

-------------------------------------------------------

-------------------------------------------------------

*"Be happy, noble heart, be blessed for all the good
thou hast done and wilt do hereafter, and let my
gratitude remain in obscurity like your good deeds."*
*— Alexandre Dumas*

Day _____ Date _____

Today I am **Grateful** for:

-------------------------------------------------------

-------------------------------------------------------

-------------------------------------------------------

-------------------------------------------------------

-------------------------------------------------------

-------------------------------------------------------

-------------------------------------------------------

Day _____ Date _____

Today I am **Grateful** for:

_____

_____

_____

_____

_____

_____

"Courtesies of a small and trivial character are the
ones which strike deepest in the grateful and
appreciating heart."
— Henry Clay

Day _____ Date _____

Today I am **Grateful** for:

_____

_____

_____

_____

_____

_____

_____

Day _____ Date _____

Today I am **Grateful** for:

------------------------------------------------

------------------------------------------------

------------------------------------------------

------------------------------------------------

------------------------------------------------

------------------------------------------------

*"A little "thank you" that you will say to someone for a "little favour" shown to you is a key to unlock the doors that hide unseen "greater favours". Learn to say "thank you" and why not?"*
— Israelmore Ayivor

Day _____ Date _____

Today I am **Grateful** for:

------------------------------------------------

------------------------------------------------

------------------------------------------------

------------------------------------------------

------------------------------------------------

------------------------------------------------

------------------------------------------------

Day _____ Date _____

Today I am **Grateful** for:

_____

_____

_____

_____

_____

_____

*"Gratitude always comes into play; research shows
that people are happier if they are grateful for the
positive things in their lives, rather than worrying
about what might be missing."*
*— Dan Buettner*

Day _____ Date _____

Today I am **Grateful** for:

_____

_____

_____

_____

_____

_____

_____

Day _____ Date _____

Today I am **Grateful** for:

---------------------------------------------------

---------------------------------------------------

---------------------------------------------------

---------------------------------------------------

---------------------------------------------------

---------------------------------------------------

*"Summoning gratitude is a sure way to get our life back on track. Opening our eyes to affirm gratitude grows the garden of our inner abundance, just as standing close to a fire eventually warms our heart."*
— *Alexandra Katehakis*

Day _____ Date _____

Today I am **Grateful** for:

---------------------------------------------------

---------------------------------------------------

---------------------------------------------------

---------------------------------------------------

---------------------------------------------------

---------------------------------------------------

---------------------------------------------------

Day _____  Date _____

Today I am **Grateful** for:

---------------------------------------------

---------------------------------------------

---------------------------------------------

---------------------------------------------

---------------------------------------------

---------------------------------------------

*"When you express gratitude for the blessings that come into your life, it not only encourages the universe to send you more, it also sees to it that those blessings remain."*
— Stephen Richards

Day _____  Date _____

Today I am **Grateful** for:

---------------------------------------------

---------------------------------------------

---------------------------------------------

---------------------------------------------

---------------------------------------------

---------------------------------------------

---------------------------------------------

Day _____ Date _____

*Today I am **Grateful** for:*

-------------------------------------------

-------------------------------------------

-------------------------------------------

-------------------------------------------

-------------------------------------------

-------------------------------------------

*"Gratitude and love are always multiplied when you give freely. It is an infinite source of contentment and prosperous energy."*
*— Jim Fargiano*

Day _____ Date _____

*Today I am **Grateful** for:*

-------------------------------------------

-------------------------------------------

-------------------------------------------

-------------------------------------------

-------------------------------------------

-------------------------------------------

Day _____ Date _____

Today I am **Grateful** for:

---------------------------------------------

---------------------------------------------

---------------------------------------------

---------------------------------------------

---------------------------------------------

---------------------------------------------

*"Don't count your blessings, let your blessings count!*
*Enjoy Life!"*
*— Bernard Kelvin Clive*

Day _____ Date _____

Today I am **Grateful** for:

---------------------------------------------

---------------------------------------------

---------------------------------------------

---------------------------------------------

---------------------------------------------

---------------------------------------------

---------------------------------------------

Day _____ Date _____

Today I am **Grateful** for:

------------------------------------------------------

------------------------------------------------------

------------------------------------------------------

------------------------------------------------------

------------------------------------------------------

------------------------------------------------------

"Most of us forget to take time for wonder, praise and
gratitude until it is almost too late. Gratitude is a
many-colored quality, reaching in all directions. It
goes out for small things and for large; it is a God-
ward going." — Faith Baldwin

Day _____ Date _____

Today I am **Grateful** for:

------------------------------------------------------

------------------------------------------------------

------------------------------------------------------

------------------------------------------------------

------------------------------------------------------

------------------------------------------------------

------------------------------------------------------

Day _____ Date _____

Today I am **Grateful** for:

_____

_____

_____

_____

_____

_____

*"No one can obtain felicity by pursuit. This explains
why one of the elements of being happy is the feeling
that a debt of gratitude is owed, a debt impossible to
pay. Now, we do not owe gratitude to ourselves. To be
conscious of gratitude is to acknowledge a gift."*
— Josef Pieper

Day _____ Date _____

Today I am **Grateful** for:

_____

_____

_____

_____

_____

_____

_____

Day _____ Date _____

Today I am *Grateful* for:

------------------------------------------------

------------------------------------------------

------------------------------------------------

------------------------------------------------

------------------------------------------------

------------------------------------------------

"When I think of how many people in this world have
it worse than I do, I realize just how blessed I really
am...... and I have to give thanks ..."
— Shannan Lea

Day _____ Date _____

Today I am *Grateful* for:

------------------------------------------------

------------------------------------------------

------------------------------------------------

------------------------------------------------

------------------------------------------------

------------------------------------------------

Day _____ Date _____

Today I am **Grateful** for:

-------------------------------------------------

-------------------------------------------------

-------------------------------------------------

-------------------------------------------------

-------------------------------------------------

-------------------------------------------------

*"I try hard to hold fast to the truth that a full and thankful heart cannot entertain great conceits. When brimming with gratitude, one's heartbeat must surely result in outgoing love, the finest emotion we can ever know."*
*— Bill W*

Day _____ Date _____

Today I am **Grateful** for:

-------------------------------------------------

-------------------------------------------------

-------------------------------------------------

-------------------------------------------------

-------------------------------------------------

-------------------------------------------------

-------------------------------------------------

Day _____ Date _____

Today I am **Grateful** for:

-----------------------------------------------

-----------------------------------------------

-----------------------------------------------

-----------------------------------------------

-----------------------------------------------

-----------------------------------------------

*"Though they only take a second to say, thank yous leave a warm feeling behind that can last for hours."*
*— Kent Allan Rees*

Day _____ Date _____

Today I am **Grateful** for:

-----------------------------------------------

-----------------------------------------------

-----------------------------------------------

-----------------------------------------------

-----------------------------------------------

-----------------------------------------------

Day _____ Date _____

Today I am **Grateful** for:

----------------------------------------------

----------------------------------------------

----------------------------------------------

----------------------------------------------

----------------------------------------------

----------------------------------------------

"Lord I thank you for the gift of breath, eyes to see,
ears to hear, tongue to taste, nose to smell, mouth to
speak, face to smile, voice to sing, body to dance, legs
to walk, mind to think and hands to write."
— Lailah Gifty Akita

Day _____ Date _____

Today I am **Grateful** for:

----------------------------------------------

----------------------------------------------

----------------------------------------------

----------------------------------------------

----------------------------------------------

----------------------------------------------

----------------------------------------------

Day _____ Date _____

Today I am **Grateful** for:

---

---

---

---

---

---

"Gratitude is the antidote for misery. When you are
counting your blessings you are too busy to be
counting your problems."
— Miya Yamanouchi

Day _____ Date _____

Today I am **Grateful** for:

---

---

---

---

---

---

Day _____ Date _____

Today I am **Grateful** for:

----------------------------------------

----------------------------------------

----------------------------------------

----------------------------------------

----------------------------------------

----------------------------------------

*"The greatest of blessings can come from what appear
to be the smallest and most insignificant of things.
Don't discredit anything or anyone. One person, one
tiny thing, one little shift can change your life in
enormous ways." — Patience W. Smith*

Day _____ Date _____

Today I am **Grateful** for:

----------------------------------------

----------------------------------------

----------------------------------------

----------------------------------------

----------------------------------------

----------------------------------------

----------------------------------------

Day _____ Date _____

Today I am **Grateful** for:

_____

_____

_____

_____

_____

_____

*"Gratitude is a divine shift in your perspective from one of separation and lack to one of unity and right mindedness. It is a choice not made from guilt but rather from a higher level of consciousness."*
*— Janet Rebhan*

Day _____ Date _____

Today I am **Grateful** for:

_____

_____

_____

_____

_____

_____

_____

Day _____ Date _____

Today I am **Grateful** for:

_____

_____

_____

_____

_____

_____

*"Gratitude is a divine emotion. It fills the heart, not to bursting; it warms it, but not to fever. I like to taste leisurely of bliss. Devoured in haste, I do not know its flavor."— Charlotte Brontë*

Day _____ Date _____

Today I am **Grateful** for:

_____

_____

_____

_____

_____

_____

Day _____ Date _____

Today I am **Grateful** for:

_____

_____

_____

_____

_____

_____

*"Road accidents, psycho killings, plane crashes abound - we don't know which day will be our last, so why not make today the happiest day and be thankful for all that we have?"*
— *Maddy Malhotra*

Day _____ Date _____

Today I am **Grateful** for:

_____

_____

_____

_____

_____

_____

Day _____ Date _____

Today I am **Grateful** for:

_____

_____

_____

_____

_____

_____

*"Gratitude for all the beauty and blessings that we
already enjoy fills our lives with abundance."*
— Debasish Mridha

Day _____ Date _____

Today I am **Grateful** for:

_____

_____

_____

_____

_____

_____

_____

Day _____ Date _____

Today I am **Grateful** for:

_____

_____

_____

_____

_____

_____

*"Be grateful for what you already have while you*
*pursue what you want."*
*— Roy Bennett*

Day _____ Date _____

Today I am **Grateful** for:

_____

_____

_____

_____

_____

_____

_____

Day _____ Date _____

Today I am **Grateful** for:

-------------------------------------------------

-------------------------------------------------

-------------------------------------------------

-------------------------------------------------

-------------------------------------------------

-------------------------------------------------

*"By talking to yourself every hour of the day, you can direct yourself to think thoughts of courage and happiness, thoughts of power and peace. By talking to yourself about the things you have to be grateful for, you can fill your mind with thoughts that soar and sing." — Dale Carnegie*

Day _____ Date _____

Today I am **Grateful** for:

-------------------------------------------------

-------------------------------------------------

-------------------------------------------------

-------------------------------------------------

-------------------------------------------------

-------------------------------------------------

-------------------------------------------------

Day _____ Date _____

Today I am **Grateful** for:

------------------------------------------

------------------------------------------

------------------------------------------

------------------------------------------

------------------------------------------

------------------------------------------

*"Practice appreciation for who you are and what you have... and allow your life to unfold in the most amazing way."*
*— Millen Livis*

Day _____ Date _____

Today I am **Grateful** for:

------------------------------------------

------------------------------------------

------------------------------------------

------------------------------------------

------------------------------------------

------------------------------------------

Day _____ Date _____

Today I am **Grateful** for:

------------------------------------------------

------------------------------------------------

------------------------------------------------

------------------------------------------------

------------------------------------------------

------------------------------------------------

*"When you overlook the small blessings in your life,
chances are that no amount of blessings would ever
make you happy."*
*— Edmond Mbiaka*

Day _____ Date _____

Today I am **Grateful** for:

------------------------------------------------

------------------------------------------------

------------------------------------------------

------------------------------------------------

------------------------------------------------

------------------------------------------------

------------------------------------------------

Day _____ Date _____

Today I am **Grateful** for:

_____

_____

_____

_____

_____

_____

"Amidst all the bacchanal and confusion in your life, find something to be grateful for, even if it is the air that you breathe and trust me, this will transform you in some small way. Gratitude is really the great multiplier." — Akosua Dardaine Edwards

Day _____ Date _____

Today I am **Grateful** for:

_____

_____

_____

_____

_____

_____

Day _____ Date _____

Today I am **Grateful** for:

_____

_____

_____

_____

_____

_____

*"Always remember people who have helped you along the way, and don't forget to lift someone up."*
*— Roy Bennett*

Day _____ Date _____

Today I am **Grateful** for:

_____

_____

_____

_____

_____

_____

Day _____ Date _____

Today I am **Grateful** for:

_____

_____

_____

_____

_____

_____

*"Gratitude, like faith, is a muscle. The more you use it, the stronger it grows, and the more power you have to use it on your behalf.. To be grateful is to find blessings in everything. This is the most powerful attitude to adopt, for there are blessings in everything." — Alan Cohen*

Day _____ Date _____

Today I am **Grateful** for:

_____

_____

_____

_____

_____

_____

_____

Day _____ Date _____

Today I am **Grateful** for:

_____

_____

_____

_____

_____

_____

*"Gratitude opens our eyes to miracles that surround us. Life's a miracle and a gift. Take every breath in gratitude"*
*— D. Denise Dianaty*

Day _____ Date _____

Today I am **Grateful** for:

_____

_____

_____

_____

_____

_____

_____

Day _____ Date _____

Today I am **Grateful** for:

---------------------------------------------------------

---------------------------------------------------------

---------------------------------------------------------

---------------------------------------------------------

---------------------------------------------------------

---------------------------------------------------------

*"Throughout the day, anytime you find yourself feeling stressed or wanting to complain, stop for 10 seconds and breathe. Count your breaths and your blessings."*
*— Jon Gordon*

Day _____ Date _____

Today I am **Grateful** for:

---------------------------------------------------------

---------------------------------------------------------

---------------------------------------------------------

---------------------------------------------------------

---------------------------------------------------------

---------------------------------------------------------

Day _____ Date _____

Today I am **Grateful** for:

_____

_____

_____

_____

_____

_____

*"Approach the goal you've set with a positive, grateful attitude, and your perception about the goal and the journey will feel less like work, and more like fun." — John Manning*

Day _____ Date _____

Today I am **Grateful** for:

_____

_____

_____

_____

_____

_____

_____

Day _____ Date _____

Today I am *Grateful* for:

-----------------------------------------------

-----------------------------------------------

-----------------------------------------------

-----------------------------------------------

-----------------------------------------------

-----------------------------------------------

*"Focus on your daily blessings, future opportunities and possibilities, and never allow your challenges, struggles, and obstacles to interfere with your peace of mind. You owe abundant happiness and success to your inner-self." — Edmond Mbiaka*

Day _____ Date _____

Today I am *Grateful* for:

-----------------------------------------------

-----------------------------------------------

-----------------------------------------------

-----------------------------------------------

-----------------------------------------------

-----------------------------------------------

Day _____ Date _____

Today I am *Grateful* for:

_____

_____

_____

_____

_____

_____

*"This morning I woke up, how blessed I am*
*Eyes to see, a voice to speak*
*Words to read and love to feel?*
*If this isn't something to be thankful for, I'm not sure*
*what is." — Nikki Rowe*

Day _____ Date _____

Today I am *Grateful* for:

_____

_____

_____

_____

_____

_____

Day _____ Date _____

Today I am **Grateful** for:

------------------------------------------------------

------------------------------------------------------

------------------------------------------------------

------------------------------------------------------

------------------------------------------------------

------------------------------------------------------

*"... most of my prayers are expressions of sheer gratitude for the fullness of my contentment."*
*— Elizabeth Gilbert*

Day _____ Date _____

Today I am **Grateful** for:

------------------------------------------------------

------------------------------------------------------

------------------------------------------------------

------------------------------------------------------

------------------------------------------------------

------------------------------------------------------

Day _____ Date _____

Today I am **Grateful** for:

------------------------------------------------------------

------------------------------------------------------------

------------------------------------------------------------

------------------------------------------------------------

------------------------------------------------------------

------------------------------------------------------------

"When you arise in the morning, give thanks for the
morning light, for your life and strength. Give
thanks for your food and the joy of living, If you see
no reason for giving thanks, the fault lies with
yourself." — Tecumseh

Day _____ Date _____

Today I am **Grateful** for:

------------------------------------------------------------

------------------------------------------------------------

------------------------------------------------------------

------------------------------------------------------------

------------------------------------------------------------

------------------------------------------------------------

Day _____ Date _____

Today I am **Grateful** for:

_____

_____

_____

_____

_____

_____

*"Gratitude is the key to manifestation, for gratitude
connects you directly to the source.
Keep your head up and heart open. And make
"Thank You" your mantra of life!
— Abhishek Kumar*

Day _____ Date _____

Today I am **Grateful** for:

_____

_____

_____

_____

_____

_____

_____

Day _____ Date _____

Today I am **Grateful** for:

_____

_____

_____

_____

_____

_____

"When last did u sit back and took an opportunity to
lookup and thank the Heavens above for blessing you
with what you have and continuing to open doors
for you every time you knock "and sometimes letting
you in through the window" because not all doors
are as beautiful on the inside as they are on the
inside" — Katlego Semusa

Day _____ Date _____

Today I am **Grateful** for:

_____

_____

_____

_____

_____

_____

_____

Day _____ Date _____

Today I am **Grateful** for:

-------------------------------------------------

-------------------------------------------------

-------------------------------------------------

-------------------------------------------------

-------------------------------------------------

-------------------------------------------------

*"The most fortunate are those who have a wonderful capacity to appreciate again and again, freshly and naively, the basic goods of life, with awe, pleasure, wonder and even ecstasy."*
*— Abraham Maslow*

Day _____ Date _____

Today I am **Grateful** for:

-------------------------------------------------

-------------------------------------------------

-------------------------------------------------

-------------------------------------------------

-------------------------------------------------

-------------------------------------------------

Day _____ Date _____

Today I am **Grateful** for:

_____

_____

_____

_____

_____

_____

*"Feeling entitled is the opposite of feeling grateful.
Gratitude opens the heart, entitlement closes it."*
— Paul Gibbons

Day _____ Date _____

Today I am **Grateful** for:

_____

_____

_____

_____

_____

_____

Day _____ Date _____

Today I am **Grateful** for:

--------------------------------------------------

--------------------------------------------------

--------------------------------------------------

--------------------------------------------------

--------------------------------------------------

--------------------------------------------------

*"Gratitude should run through our veins, it should reside in us, it should live in our bones as long we live."*
*— Euginia Herlihy*

Day _____ Date _____

Today I am **Grateful** for:

--------------------------------------------------

--------------------------------------------------

--------------------------------------------------

--------------------------------------------------

--------------------------------------------------

--------------------------------------------------

Day _____ Date _____

Today I am **Grateful** for:

------------------------------------------------

------------------------------------------------

------------------------------------------------

------------------------------------------------

------------------------------------------------

------------------------------------------------

*"The more we express thanks, the more gratitude we feel. The more gratitude we feel, the more we express thanks. It's circular, and it leads to a happier life."*
*— Steve Goodier*

Day _____ Date _____

Today I am **Grateful** for:

------------------------------------------------

------------------------------------------------

------------------------------------------------

------------------------------------------------

------------------------------------------------

------------------------------------------------

------------------------------------------------

Day _____ Date _____

Today I am **Grateful** for:

_____

_____

_____

_____

_____

_____

*"If I do not feel a sense of joy in God's creation, if I forget to offer the world back to God with thankfulness, I have advanced very little upon the Way. I have not yet learnt to be truly human. For it is only through thanksgiving that I can become myself." — Kallistos Ware*

Day _____ Date _____

Today I am **Grateful** for:

_____

_____

_____

_____

_____

_____

Day _____ Date _____

Today I am **Grateful** for:

------------------------------------------------

------------------------------------------------

------------------------------------------------

------------------------------------------------

------------------------------------------------

------------------------------------------------

*"There is no prescription for finding moments of gratitude in every day; there is simply the choice."*
*— Gillian Deacon*

Day _____ Date _____

Today I am **Grateful** for:

------------------------------------------------

------------------------------------------------

------------------------------------------------

------------------------------------------------

------------------------------------------------

------------------------------------------------

Day _____ Date _____

Today I am **Grateful** for:

-------------------------------------------------

-------------------------------------------------

-------------------------------------------------

-------------------------------------------------

-------------------------------------------------

-------------------------------------------------

*"We all feel better when we are grateful. There is great wisdom in understanding that no matter the situation, there is always something for which we can choose to be grateful."*
*— Andy Andrews*

Day _____ Date _____

Today I am **Grateful** for:

-------------------------------------------------

-------------------------------------------------

-------------------------------------------------

-------------------------------------------------

-------------------------------------------------

-------------------------------------------------

-------------------------------------------------

Day _____ Date _____

Today I am **Grateful** for:

---------------------------------------------------

---------------------------------------------------

---------------------------------------------------

---------------------------------------------------

---------------------------------------------------

---------------------------------------------------

*"The most beautiful moments in life are moments*
*when you are expressing your joy, not when you are*
*seeking it."*
*— Jaggi Vasudev*

Day _____ Date _____

Today I am **Grateful** for:

---------------------------------------------------

---------------------------------------------------

---------------------------------------------------

---------------------------------------------------

---------------------------------------------------

---------------------------------------------------

Day _____ Date _____

Today I am **Grateful** for:

_____

_____

_____

_____

_____

_____

"Grow in a way without losing much of our inner
childlike deep senses embracing truthful, pure,
simple relief of appreciation and gratitude."
— Angelica Hopes

Day _____ Date _____

Today I am **Grateful** for:

_____

_____

_____

_____

_____

_____

Day _____ Date _____

Today I am **Grateful** for:

_____

_____

_____

_____

_____

_____

*"Feeling grateful is good; showing appreciation to those you feel grateful to is sublime."*
*— Andy Lacroix*

Day _____ Date _____

Today I am **Grateful** for:

_____

_____

_____

_____

_____

_____

_____

Day _____ Date _____

Today I am **Grateful** for:

_____

_____

_____

_____

_____

_____

"Be grateful for life. Show gratitude to others,
whether it's verbally or energetically, it has
the same effect."
— Kasi Kaye Iliopoulos

Day _____ Date _____

Today I am **Grateful** for:

_____

_____

_____

_____

_____

_____

Day _____ Date _____

Today I am *Grateful* for:

-------------------------------------------------

-------------------------------------------------

-------------------------------------------------

-------------------------------------------------

-------------------------------------------------

-------------------------------------------------

"I count myself lucky, having long ago won a lottery
paid to me in seven sunrises a week for life."
— Robert Brault

Day _____ Date _____

Today I am *Grateful* for:

-------------------------------------------------

-------------------------------------------------

-------------------------------------------------

-------------------------------------------------

-------------------------------------------------

-------------------------------------------------

-------------------------------------------------

Day _____ Date _____

Today I am **Grateful** for:

-----------------------------------------------------------

-----------------------------------------------------------

-----------------------------------------------------------

-----------------------------------------------------------

-----------------------------------------------------------

-----------------------------------------------------------

1. Woke up ✓
2. Air to breath ✓
3. Food to eat ✓
4. Roof over head ✓
...yep, it's a Good day!"
— Russell Kyle

Day _____ Date _____

Today I am **Grateful** for:

-----------------------------------------------------------

-----------------------------------------------------------

-----------------------------------------------------------

-----------------------------------------------------------

-----------------------------------------------------------

-----------------------------------------------------------

Day _____ Date _____

Today I am **Grateful** for:

_____

_____

_____

_____

_____

_____

*"The Power of Thank You goes a very long way! Its healing embodiment of gratitude is a key element to living a happier life."*
*— Angie Karan Krezos*

Day _____ Date _____

Today I am **Grateful** for:

_____

_____

_____

_____

_____

_____

Day _____ Date _____

Today I am **Grateful** for:

_____

_____

_____

_____

_____

_____

*"Nothing is so fundamental to the spiritual life as
learning to give thanks."
— Gordon T. Smith*

Day _____ Date _____

Today I am **Grateful** for:

_____

_____

_____

_____

_____

_____

Day _____ Date _____

Today I am **Grateful** for:

---------------------------------------------------

---------------------------------------------------

---------------------------------------------------

---------------------------------------------------

---------------------------------------------------

---------------------------------------------------

*"When you open to your heart, your entire world changes--it opens up around you. You see yourself as part of a friendly universe, one that is full of possibility, one that is generating and regenerating a positive energy." — Baptist de Pape*

Day _____ Date _____

Today I am **Grateful** for:

---------------------------------------------------

---------------------------------------------------

---------------------------------------------------

---------------------------------------------------

---------------------------------------------------

---------------------------------------------------

Day _____ Date _____

Today I am **Grateful** for:

_____

_____

_____

_____

_____

_____

*"You must love yourself first to the soul
of your aura..."*
*— Jennifer Pierre*

Day _____ Date _____

Today I am **Grateful** for:

_____

_____

_____

_____

_____

_____

Day _____ Date _____

Today I am **Grateful** for:

_____

_____

_____

_____

_____

_____

*"The height of our success is marked at the depth of
our gratitude."*
*— Terry Crouson*

Day _____ Date _____

Today I am **Grateful** for:

_____

_____

_____

_____

_____

_____

Day _____ Date _____

Today I am **Grateful** for:

_____

_____

_____

_____

_____

_____

*"If the heights of our joy are measured by the depths
of our gratitude, and gratitude is but a way of
seeing, a spiritual perspective of smallness might offer
a vital way of seeing especially conducive to
gratitude"* — Ann Voskamp

Day _____ Date _____

Today I am **Grateful** for:

_____

_____

_____

_____

_____

_____

Day _____ Date _____

Today I am **Grateful** for:

-----------------------------------------------

-----------------------------------------------

-----------------------------------------------

-----------------------------------------------

-----------------------------------------------

-----------------------------------------------

*"When your heart aligns with the truth of its energy, GRATITUDE sings your name, LOVE flows freely, and every bit of your being is awakened, breathing and moving in perfect HARMONY."*
— *Angie Karan Krezos*

Day _____ Date _____

Today I am **Grateful** for:

-----------------------------------------------

-----------------------------------------------

-----------------------------------------------

-----------------------------------------------

-----------------------------------------------

-----------------------------------------------

----------------------------------------

Day _____     Date _____

Today I am **Grateful** for:

----------------------------------------

----------------------------------------

----------------------------------------

----------------------------------------

----------------------------------------

----------------------------------------

*"Just as thoughts, send out vibrations to which there
is a creative and attractive power, gratitude
stimulates the field of etheric energy that surrounds
you on a subtle level to bring into your life more of
what brings you joy."— Genevieve Gerard*

Day _____     Date _____

Today I am **Grateful** for:

----------------------------------------

----------------------------------------

----------------------------------------

----------------------------------------

----------------------------------------

----------------------------------------

Day _____ Date _____

Today I am **Grateful** for:

------------------------------------------------------------

------------------------------------------------------------

------------------------------------------------------------

------------------------------------------------------------

------------------------------------------------------------

------------------------------------------------------------

"Never let them try out this gratitude, for they would
immediately discover that it supplies the first and
most important component to happiness:
Contentment."
— Geoffrey Wood

Day _____ Date _____

Today I am **Grateful** for:

------------------------------------------------------------

------------------------------------------------------------

------------------------------------------------------------

------------------------------------------------------------

------------------------------------------------------------

---------------------------------

---------------------------------

Day _____ Date _____

Today I am **Grateful** for:

---------------------------------

---------------------------------

---------------------------------

---------------------------------

---------------------------------

---------------------------------

*"The good news is that being in gratitude does not
require time and money. All it requires is an
attitude of being grateful."*
*— Vishwas Chavan*

Day _____ Date _____

Today I am **Grateful** for:

---------------------------------

---------------------------------

---------------------------------

---------------------------------

---------------------------------

---------------------------------

Day _____ Date _____

Today I am **Grateful** for:

_____

_____

_____

_____

_____

_____

*"Love is such a deep gratitude. When you are truly in love with life, every breath you take is gratitude."*
*— Bryant McGill*

Day _____ Date _____

Today I am **Grateful** for:

_____

_____

_____

_____

_____

_____

Day _____ Date _____

Today I am **Grateful** for:

_____

_____

_____

_____

_____

_____

*"Being able to appreciate who we are and what we
have in the now is an easy way to journey
through this life."*
*— Raphael Zernoff*

Day _____ Date _____

Today I am **Grateful** for:

_____

_____

_____

_____

_____

_____

Day _____ Date _____

Today I am **Grateful** for:

------------------------------------------------

------------------------------------------------

------------------------------------------------

------------------------------------------------

------------------------------------------------

------------------------------------------------

*"As we express our gratitude, we must never forget
that the highest appreciation is not to utter words,
but to live by them."*
*— John F. Kennedy*

Day _____ Date _____

Today I am **Grateful** for:

------------------------------------------------

------------------------------------------------

------------------------------------------------

------------------------------------------------

------------------------------------------------

------------------------------------------------

Day _____ Date _____

Today I am **Grateful** for:

---------------------------------------------

---------------------------------------------

---------------------------------------------

---------------------------------------------

---------------------------------------------

---------------------------------------------

*"Gratitude is the heart of humility, and humility is
the path to peace, love, and understanding."*
*— Justin Young*

Day _____ Date _____

Today I am **Grateful** for:

---------------------------------------------

---------------------------------------------

---------------------------------------------

---------------------------------------------

---------------------------------------------

---------------------------------------------

Day _____ Date _____

Today I am **Grateful** for:

_____

_____

_____

_____

_____

_____

*"How would your life be different if you celebrated
the things in your life that you do have instead of
lamenting things that you don't? Let today be the
day you embrace gratitude and appreciation and
let go of entitlement and expectation."*
*— Steve Maraboli*

Day _____ Date _____

Today I am **Grateful** for:

_____

_____

_____

_____

_____

_____

Day _____ Date _____

Today I am **Grateful** for:

_____

_____

_____

_____

_____

_____

*"With all respect to your religion or world-view —*
*thank God, thank the universe, thank evolutionary*
*processes — the keyword is "thank" — just have some*
*gratitude and be thankful."*
*— Bryant McGill*

Day _____ Date _____

Today I am **Grateful** for:

_____

_____

_____

_____

_____

_____

Day _____ Date _____

Today I am **Grateful** for:

_____

_____

_____

_____

_____

_____

*"Embrace the change you desperately need. Tear down your walls and show gratitude for little things." — J Loren Norris*

Day _____ Date _____

Today I am **Grateful** for:

_____

_____

_____

_____

_____

_____

Day _____ Date _____

Today I am **Grateful** for:

_____

_____

_____

_____

_____

_____

*"Gratitude is an excellent attitude which can lift you
to a greater altitude if you put it on as a vesture."*
*— S. E. Entsua-Mensah*

Day _____ Date _____

Today I am **Grateful** for:

_____

_____

_____

_____

_____

_____

Day _____ Date _____

Today I am **Grateful** for:

_____

_____

_____

_____

_____

_____

*"The moment that you give gratitude is the moment that you find happiness. The moment that you lose gratitude your happiness will vanish and slip through your fingers" — Rasheed Ogunlaru*

Day _____ Date _____

Today I am **Grateful** for:

_____

_____

_____

_____

_____

_____

------------------------------------

Day _____  Date _____

Today I am **Grateful** for:

------------------------------------

------------------------------------

------------------------------------

------------------------------------

------------------------------------

------------------------------------

*"Gratitude is not just a word; it is a way of life."*
— *Rob Martin*

Day _____  Date _____

Today I am **Grateful** for:

------------------------------------

------------------------------------

------------------------------------

------------------------------------

------------------------------------

------------------------------------

Day _____ Date _____

Today I am **Grateful** for:

------------------------------------------------

------------------------------------------------

------------------------------------------------

------------------------------------------------

------------------------------------------------

------------------------------------------------

*"I live by three simple words: compassion, love and gratitude. We need to act on these three words daily. Doing so will irrevocably change your world."*
*— Julian Pencilliah*

Day _____ Date _____

Today I am **Grateful** for:

------------------------------------------------

------------------------------------------------

------------------------------------------------

------------------------------------------------

------------------------------------------------

------------------------------------------------

Day _____ Date _____

Today I am **Grateful** for:

_____

_____

_____

_____

_____

_____

"This is a wonderful day. I've never seen
this one before."
— Maya Angelou

Day _____ Date _____

Today I am **Grateful** for:

_____

_____

_____

_____

_____

_____

Day _____ Date _____

Today I am **Grateful** for:

_____

_____

_____

_____

_____

_____

*"Find magic in the little things, and the big things
you always expected will start to show up."*
*— Isa Zapata*

Day _____ Date _____

Today I am **Grateful** for:

_____

_____

_____

_____

_____

_____

Day _____ Date _____

Today I am **Grateful** for:

_____

_____

_____

_____

_____

_____

*"If we all counted our blessings and then shared*
*them with our neighbors, near and far,*
*all our lives would be richer."*
*— Janet Autherine*

Day _____ Date _____

Today I am **Grateful** for:

_____

_____

_____

_____

_____

_____

Day _____ Date _____

Today I am **Grateful** for:

_____

_____

_____

_____

_____

_____

*"Amazement + Gratitude + Openness + Appreciation =*
*an irresistible field of energy"*
*— Frederick Dodson*

Day _____ Date _____

Today I am **Grateful** for:

_____

_____

_____

_____

_____

_____

Day _____ Date _____

Today I am **Grateful** for:

---------------------------------------------------

---------------------------------------------------

---------------------------------------------------

---------------------------------------------------

---------------------------------------------------

---------------------------------------------------

*"You simply will not be the same person two months*
*from now after consciously giving thanks each day*
*for the abundance that exists in your life."*
*— Sarah Ban Breathnach*

Day _____ Date _____

Today I am **Grateful** for:

---------------------------------------------------

---------------------------------------------------

---------------------------------------------------

---------------------------------------------------

---------------------------------------------------

---------------------------------------------------

Day _____ Date _____

Today I am **Grateful** for:

_____

_____

_____

_____

_____

_____

*"Everyday gratitude sweetens what appears flavorless*
*and brightens all that appears dim."*
*— Amy Leigh Mercree*

Day _____ Date _____

Today I am **Grateful** for:

_____

_____

_____

_____

_____

_____

Day _____ Date _____

Today I am **Grateful** for:

_____

_____

_____

_____

_____

_____

*"Every day, tell at least one person something you like, admire, or appreciate about them."*
*— Richard Carlson*

Day _____ Date _____

Today I am **Grateful** for:

_____

_____

_____

_____

_____

_____

Day _____ Date _____

Today I am **Grateful** for:

_____

_____

_____

_____

_____

_____

*"In life, as in knitting, don't leave loose ends. Take
the time to thank the people who matter in your life."*
*— Reba Linker*

Day _____ Date _____

Today I am **Grateful** for:

_____

_____

_____

_____

_____

_____

Day _____ Date _____

Today I am **Grateful** for:

-------------------------------------------------

-------------------------------------------------

-------------------------------------------------

-------------------------------------------------

-------------------------------------------------

-------------------------------------------------

*"Gratitude makes you a better, stronger, wiser person.*
*Ingratitude makes you a negative, angry, miserable*
*person. Which person do you choose to be?"*
*— Tanya Masse*

Day _____ Date _____

Today I am **Grateful** for:

-------------------------------------------------

-------------------------------------------------

-------------------------------------------------

-------------------------------------------------

-------------------------------------------------

-------------------------------------------------

Day _____ Date _____

Today I am **Grateful** for:

---------------------------------------------------

---------------------------------------------------

---------------------------------------------------

---------------------------------------------------

---------------------------------------------------

---------------------------------------------------

*"What I've learned is there's a scientifically proven phenomenon that's attached to gratitude, and that if you consciously take note of what is good in your life, quantifiable benefits happen."*
— Deborah Norville

Day _____ Date _____

Today I am **Grateful** for:

---------------------------------------------------

---------------------------------------------------

---------------------------------------------------

---------------------------------------------------

---------------------------------------------------

---------------------------------------------------

Day _____ Date _____

Today I am **Grateful** for:

_____

_____

_____

_____

_____

_____

*"Gratitude is not something idyllic that comes when
all good things line up to be counted. Gratitude is
there all the time waiting to be focused on."*
— Antonia Montoya

Day _____ Date _____

Today I am **Grateful** for:

_____

_____

_____

_____

_____

_____

Day _____ Date _____

Today I am **Grateful** for:

------------------------------------------------

------------------------------------------------

------------------------------------------------

------------------------------------------------

------------------------------------------------

------------------------------------------------

*"If we do not feel grateful for what we already have,*
*what makes us think we would be happy with more?"*
*— John A. Passaro*

Day _____ Date _____

Today I am **Grateful** for:

------------------------------------------------

------------------------------------------------

------------------------------------------------

------------------------------------------------

------------------------------------------------

------------------------------------------------

Day _____ Date _____

Today I am **Grateful** for:

_____

_____

_____

_____

_____

_____

*"Thankfulness is the beginning of gratitude.*
*Gratitude is the completion of thankfulness.*
*Thankfulness may consist merely of words.*
*Gratitude is shown in acts."*
*— Henri-Frédéric Amiel*

Day _____ Date _____

Today I am **Grateful** for:

_____

_____

_____

_____

_____

_____

*Need another 5 Minute Gratitude Journal?*
*Visit www.blankbooksnjournals.com*

CPSIA information can be obtained
at www.ICGtesting.com
Printed in the USA
LVOW01s2247170316
479683LV00033B/908/P